A HISTORY OF THE
WORLD IN 100
LIMERICKS

There was an Old Geezer called Caesar

Mick Twister

PITKIN

First published in the United Kingdom in 2013
by Portico
This edition first published in the United Kingdom
in 2021 by
B.T. Batsford
43 Great Ormond Street
London WC1N 3HZ

An imprint of B.T. Batsford Holdings Limited

ISBN: 9781841659404

A CIP catalogue record for this book is available from
the British Library.

10 9 8 7 6 5 4 3 2 1

Reproduction by Rival Colour Ltd, UK
Printed and bound by Vivar Printing Sdn Bhd, Malaysia

This book can be ordered direct from the publisher at www.batsford.com,
or try your local bookshop

CONTENTS

A NOTE ON SOURCES

The further in history you go
The harder the facts are to know
'Cos the things that you're li'ble
To read in the Bible
It ain't necessarily so.

(With apologies to George and Ira Gershwin)

HELLO THERE!

The bard said that wit's soul is brevity*
So writing a history with levity
Must by definition
Mean sins of omission
Because of our planet's longevity.

Trying to reflect the history of the world in 100 limericks is an absurd task, and I apologise if my selection of events seems spurious or idiosyncratic, Euro- or Anglo-centric, or merely ec-centric. Many important historical topics were left out or skimmed over simply because I couldn't get any humour out of them, or find a decent rhyme (never mind an indecent one, which is always preferable).

*See pp.50–51.

The form naturally lends itself to the Great Man (or Woman) school of history. That's because limericks aren't quite as good at analysing patterns of land tenure in medieval European agrarian societies as they are at mocking William the Conqueror's prodigiously large belly. Long before Edward Lear, limericks were part of an oral tradition that used humour to prick the egos of the pompous and powerful.

Many of the limericks revolve around well-known anecdotes, for which in a lot of cases there is not a shred of evidence. But that in itself often says something about how those subsequently recording history wanted to remember this or that person of note.

GLOBALISATION

There once was a great ball of gas
That cooled to a big solid mass,
And that was the birth
Of the planet named Earth —
We weren't there to see it, alas.

Well, you have to start somewhere, don't you? So, skipping rapidly over the first two thirds of the 13.75 billion years since the Big Bang created the Universe, let's pick up the story about four and a half billion years ago.

A big rotating cloud of gas and dust, mainly hydrogen and helium, resolved itself into the Solar System, with rings around the Sun tending to form into gassy clumps – one of which was the Earth.

After all that excitement, Earth felt it was time to settle down and start forming some solid foundations for future life – like rocks and water. A place with a bit of atmosphere. We have no eyewitness testimony, of course. But scientists reckon it took up to a billion years to create the kind of conditions in which a self-respecting proto-cell of living matter might consider replicating.

THEYNEVERSAURUS

The dinosaurs like Allosaurus
Died out quite a long time before us
Which worked in our favour —
We've such a nice flavour,
I doubt that they'd want to ignore us.

Over time, the simple organisms that were the Earth's early inhabitants had kids who were smarter than them: some became plants; the best swimmers got to be fish; the more mobile ones were insects; while the good all-rounders turned into amphibians.

But the ones who ate all their greens – or their meat, depending on the species – grew up to be dinosaurs, and they're the early Earth inhabitants who fascinate us the most. They ran the show throughout the Jurassic and Cretaceous periods, from about 200 million to about 65 million years ago.

The largest dinosaurs, such as Diplodocus and Argentinosaurus, were 18 metres tall, but vegetarian. Carnivores like Allosaurus and Tyrannosaurus Rex were midgets by comparison – probably only the size of a double-decker bus!

HOMO ON THE RANGE

Homo sapiens came on the scene
In Africa, mid-Pleistocene,
Though Homo erectus
Appears to connect us
With earlier apes there had been.

Quite a long time after the dinosaurs had died out, we decided it was safe to evolve. It's probably about 5–7 million years since human ancestors diverged from chimpanzee ones, but modern humans only evolved about 200,000 years ago, which to a palaeontologist is almost as recent as the 1970s.

There were a few early versions of *Homo* for whom things didn't work so well. There's disagreement over whether *Homo erectus* was one of these (stop sniggering at the back, it means 'standing up man'), but *Homo neanderthalis* certainly was.

We tend to view the Neanderthals as big thickos, but it now seems their brains may have been bigger than ours. And they were stronger. So how did we gain the upper hand evolution-wise? We must just have been meaner.

OLD MASTERS

There were some old folks in Lascaux,
A terribly long time ago,
Who drew on the walls
Of their cavernous halls.
Why they did it, we don't rightly know.

Various things set humans apart from our close relatives as we continued to evolve. Use of tools was one, and art another. As long as 32,000 years ago, early humans started to scratch marks on the walls of caves, and even to colour with charcoal and ochre.

Lascaux, in south-west France, is one of the best-known sites for cave paintings, with 2,000 figures, including horses and bulls, dating from about 17,300 years ago. And this primitive European school of art had counterparts in Asia and South America. Not being easily able to attend each other's gallery openings, they appear to have evolved independently.

We don't know why they did it. But it certainly made sense to paint in caves, where the cool dark atmosphere has allowed them to survive a lot longer than one of Damien Hirst's pickled sharks.

THE FIRST ACCOUNTANTS

Some of the earliest writing
Was used to tell stories of fighting,
While ancient Sumerians
Logged their experience
And their accounts (less exciting).

Those old cave paintings may have been used to tell stories, even if the plots didn't get much beyond 'man meets deer, man kills deer, man eats deer'. But it was a short step from that to pictograms – communication using pictures instead of words.

Writing proper seems to have been invented in several parts of the world quite separately, but the first writers whose work we've been able to decode were the Sumerians of Mesopotamia – in modern Iraq – around 3500 BC.

Now, tales of great victories and epic journeys could not only be told *ad nauseam* around the camp-fire or banqueting table, they could be written down for posterity. But the Sumerians were also traders, and writing enabled them to keep business records – not tablet-turners, perhaps, but thrilling to archaeologists.

GIZA GEEZER

There was an old pharaoh from Giza,
Some 2,000 years before Caesar,
Had a pyramid built
So his flesh wouldn't wilt,
As we'd yet to invent the deep-freezer.

About 800 miles away, another great civilisation was growing up along the Nile, where the ancient Egyptians created lasting artworks, buildings and monuments that still fill museums around the world.

Their bodies were, of course, still vulnerable to the ravages of time. But the Egyptians believed not only that the soul lived on, but that it needed the body. So they developed ways of embalming corpses, mummifying them and storing them with lots of valuable stuff they might need, all in airtight tombs under pyramids. The biggest was the grand pyramid at Giza, built for the pharaoh Khufu around 2500 BC.

It's now thought that the pyramids weren't built by slaves, but rather by free labourers, who were well-paid in bread, meat and large amounts of beer. One crew of builders wrote their name on the wall of the toilet area – 'The Drunkards'.

ROCK OF AGES

The Britons of Salisbury Plain
Used all of their might and their main
To build a stone circle,
Not knowing their work'll
Stand 4,000 years in the rain.

While the Egyptians were building pyramids, their counterparts in Bronze Age Britain were laying the foundations of rave culture. The massive stone circle known as Stonehenge, now a focal point for new age hippy types, was built somewhere between 3000 and 2000 BC with stones carried 150 miles from South Wales.

Ever since, people have tried to figure out how and why. The most sustained speculation surrounds the alignment of some of the stones with the position of the sun at the summer solstice – was it a calendar of sorts, or a location for sun worship?

The trouble is, you are lucky if you actually see the sun on any given day in Britain, Midsummer or not. So half the time the ancient Brits must have sat there watching raindrops bounce off the bluestones. And feeling cursed by the gods.

SMILEY CYRUS

There was an old fellow named Cyrus
Whose tolerance still can inspire us.
He let people be
And he set the Jews free
(Or so we read in the papyrus).

Back where the sun was hot enough to bake clay, Cyrus the Great of Persia may have written the first ever declaration of human rights. It wasn't actually on papyrus (that was poetic licence), but on a clay cylinder, probably so it would last longer – and it did. Written in 539 BC, it was found in the ruins of Babylon in 1879.

The Cyrus cylinder set out policies on religious tolerance and the abolition of slavery, and sure enough, Cyrus released thousands of Jews who had been held captive in Babylon for years.

But as well as human rights, he may have pioneered chemical warfare – according to Herodotus, he defeated Lydia's King Croesus by deploying a herd of camels so smelly that the Lydian horses turned tail and fled.

GREEK GEEKS

There were some top thinkers in Attica –
Pythagoras, top mathematicker,
Plato, Hippocrates,
Xenophon, Socrates
(He could have been democraticker).

While Persia pioneered human rights, ancient Greece is seen as the cradle of democracy, and of philosophy – which 2,500 years ago covered most branches of knowledge. Pythagoras is best known for the theorem about right-angled triangles, which he may or may not have invented. But he was also big on metaphysics.

Hippocrates pretty much founded medicine – doctors still swear by him. Plato was more of a 'true' philosopher, musing about the reality of the evidence of our senses and stuff. He also looked at politics, arguing that a bad tyranny was better than a bad democracy, because at least only one person was to blame.

Socrates was accused of links to the 30 tyrants who took over in 404 BC. So if Greece was the cradle of democracy, its guardians weren't averse to giving the infant a firm slap when it misbehaved.

MAKE LOVE AND WAR

Macedonian King Alexander
Excelled as an army commander
Brought up as a thinker
He turned sex-mad drinker
(This may attract charges of slander).

Alexander the Great also studied philosophy, but is remembered as a great military commander. By the time of his death aged 33, he had led a sometimes-reluctant army as far as India.

It's well known that Alexander liked a drink, but his attitude to sex was less clear-cut. He's often portrayed as a great womaniser, but though he married twice, his closest relationship appears to have been with his male childhood friend Hephaistion, who may well have been his lover.

People still get touchy about this; a group of Greek lawyers threatened to sue Oliver Stone for his gay portrayal of Alexander in his 2004 film. And the former Yugoslav Republic of Macedonia and Greece argue over who has the better claim to him. But during his life Al preferred Persia anyway, so Iran probably has.

HISTORY IS BUNK I

The Emperor Qin (pronounced Chin)
Thought history books were a sin,
So he built a big pyre
And set them on fire —
Just his favourites didn't go in.

Another conqueror was Qin Shi Huang, who in 221 BC became the first emperor to rule the whole of China.

Qin banned all of China's '100 schools of thought' apart from his favoured school of legalism, and ordered all books to be burned except for useful ones such as those on war, agriculture and medicine. Terrified of death, Qin was tricked by two alchemists who promised him eternal life, so he took his revenge by ordering 460 scholars to be buried alive.

On the plus side, he built the Great Wall of China — well, thousands of labourers built it, many of whom died in the process. He was also responsible for the mausoleum with its famous Terracotta Army, supposed to protect him after death — which suggests he eventually had to accept his own mortality.

A GEEZER CALLED CAESAR

The emperor Julius Caesar
To Romans, was quite a crowd-pleaser.
But Brutus et al –
His bloody best pal –
Conspired to murder the geezer.

In Europe, Rome took over from Greece as the dominant power. And the Romans borrowed many things from the Greeks – adopted their customs and their Gods, and studied their philosophers.

The Romans also took up the idea of democracy. From 500 BC, for about half a century, Rome was a republic, with a senate and legislative assemblies. But society was divided into patricians and plebeians, who vied for power.

Julius Caesar used the plebs to take power, effectively turning the republic into an empire, with himself appointed dictator for life in 44 BC. But as Gore Vidal said, 'Every time a friend succeeds, I die a little', and I guess that's how Caesar's backstabbing best mate Brutus felt about it. Except that he and his co-conspirators made sure it was Caesar who died – a lot.

MINE'S A SNAKEBITE

There once was an ancient Egyptian
Whose beauty defied all description.
She was driven to take
Her life with a snake
Not having strong drugs on prescription.

When Caesar was assassinated, his part-time lover Cleopatra was so upset that she had to be consoled by Mark Antony.

So was Cleo as good-looking as she's cracked up to be? She certainly had pulling power, but then she was probably the richest woman in the Mediterranean. And her seductive arts were legendary – she picked Mark Antony up on a posh barge, and had herself rolled up in a carpet and delivered to Caesar. Plus all those baths in asses' milk must have given her a complexion to die for.

Cleopatra knew all about stuff like that: she wrote a medical treatise with advice on everything from foundation to pharmacology. So when in 30 BC she'd lost everything – her lovers and her empire – she knew just which venomous snake to pick for a swift death.

MUSIC TO WATCH FLAMES BY

There was an old fellow called Nero
Whose ratings in Rome sank to zero,
When he started a fire
Then played on his lyre,
When he should have been playing the hero.

The Caesars that followed Julius decided to see how much they could get away with in terms of debauchery. Which, when you have absolute power, is quite a lot – orgies, incest, poisoning relatives and appointing horses to positions of power, for example.

Nero is best known, of course, for fiddling while Rome burned. Which is nonsense, as they didn't have violins then – it was a lyre. As for the Great Fire of 64 AD, many Romans suspected him of starting it to make way for the palace he built on the site.

So Nero needed an alternative scapegoat, preferably in the form of a minority group he could pick on, and that's when the Roman persecution of the new heretic sect called the Christians really got going: the pyromaniac Nero allegedly set Christians on fire in the garden at night to provide light.

YOU FEELING OKAY, HUN?

A chap named Attila the Hun,
With a sizeable empire to run,
Spent years fighting Rome
Before dying at home
Of a nosebleed — or so it was spun.

As Rome lost its grip, opportunities opened up for other conquerors. One was Attila the Hun, whose empire spanned most of Eastern Europe, including a chunk of Russia.

In the 440s he took control of most of the Balkans from Rome (now a Christian empire), then his armies fought their way across Germany, Belgium, France and northern Italy, but failed to take Rome itself after Leo I begged, bribed or otherwise persuaded him to leave it alone.

After all that, Attila died at home in what's now Hungary. A Roman account said he had a fatal nosebleed on his wedding night, brought on by excessive drinking. But was that a cover for his assassination by the Byzantine emperor? After all, what better way to diminish a warrior than by giving him a humiliating death.

MUSCLES FROM BRUSSELS

Charlemagne, the King of the Franks,
Conquered Europe to earn the Pope's thanks.
His men used their muscles
Where nowadays Brussels
Holds sway through the power of banks.

Charlemagne (pronounced 'shar-le-manyer', just in case anyone suspects my limerick of failing to scan) is a great popular hero in France, credited with uniting the warring tribes of Europe for the first time since the collapse of the Roman Empire.

After unifying France in 768, he moved on to neighbouring countries, turning the pagan Saxons of Germany into either Christians or dead pagans. So the Pope created for him the post of Holy Roman Emperor.

Born in Belgium, Chazzer ruled over what today is France, Germany, the Benelux countries and Italy. The next time these six were united was in 1959, when they signed the Treaty of – wait for it – Rome, which led to the European Union. But Charlemagne's EU successors rely on fiscal might, rather than physical.

BODY OF EVIDENCE

There was an old Pope known as Stephen
Whose story takes quite some believin'.
He dug up a stiff,
Ignoring the whiff
And put it on trial to get even.

In the first millennium AD, the Christians in Rome went from being the kids everyone picked on to ruling the school. And the Popes in Rome in the Middle Ages were a pretty powerful bunch.

Like the Caesars, some were corrupted by power. In the tenth century John XII's lovers included his niece and his father's concubine; in the eleventh century Benedict IX was accused of sodomy and bestiality and holding orgies; and in the fifteenth century Paul II allegedly died in bed with a male prostitute.

The maddest Pope was the ninth century's Stephen VI, who is remembered for a bizarre act of retribution: he had the rotting corpse of his predecessor dug up, dressed in papal robes and put on trial. The ex-Pope was found guilty of wrongly assuming office and had three fingers cut off. Bet that taught him a lesson.

AM-ERIK-A

The Vikings, the Danes and the Norse
Took large parts of Europe by force.
But for one pal of Erik a
Part of America
Loomed when the wind changed his course.

Bjarni Herjolfsson and Leif Eriksson deserve to be just as well known as Christopher Columbus. In so far as any Europeans 'found' America (bearing in mind the native Americans hadn't actually lost it), these Vikings did, about 500 years before him.

In the tenth century the Vikings ruled the waves. Tired of Iceland, which was actually quite green, Erik the Red found a properly icy land further north, and cunningly called it Greenland, to entice others there.

Bjarni got blown off course en route to Greenland, and came back with tales of a strange wooded land. That got Erik's son Leif interested, and in around 1000 AD, he landed in Newfoundland. So why did Leif leave? One saga says his men offered cow's milk to the lactose-intolerant Native Americans, who threw up, and promptly turned on the Vikings. Oh, for a carton of soya milk!

STONKERED CONQUEROR

All-conquering William the Bastard
Found one thing he never quite mastered.
With kilos to lose,
He tried sticking to booze
But fell off his charger while plastered.

Some Vikings settled in northern France, and it was from here William the Bastard (nothing personal, it's just his father and mother weren't married) attacked England in 1066. After the Battle of Hastings he acquired the more dignified title of William the Conqueror.

Towards the end of his days, William the Large was so fat that he had trouble getting on his horse, and it's said he tried an alcohol-only diet to lose weight. Whether drunk in charge of a charger or not, he crashed at Mantes and ruptured his intestines.

They had such trouble cramming William the Bloated into his coffin that his swollen belly burst, causing a stench that even the cheese-loving Normans found unbearable. Unlike the Battle of Hastings, this event was not recorded on the Bayeux Tapestry.

SALADIN SANE

A bloke called Saladin, a Kurd
Was known as a man of his word,
A chivalrous knight
Who was mostly all right
(Though doubtless some errors occurred).

Crusading was not a pretty sight: the main way to prove the superiority of one's religion seemed to be to out-kill the other lot.

But the Muslim sultan Saladin and his crusader counterpart Richard the Lionheart are said to have had a good rapport (considering they almost certainly never met). Theirs was a strong relationship of mutual respect and knightly chivalry – with Saladin even sending Richard gifts on occasion.

Saladin could be as ruthless a killer as the next man – or just kill the next man if necessary – but when he took Jerusalem he agreed to let those inside go for a ransom. He even let some of them off when they pleaded poverty. And when he died in 1193, he didn't have enough for his own funeral, having given his money to the poor – unlike a later son of Tikrit, Saddam Hussein.

BUGGERED FROM THE START

The Cathars of southwestern France
Were put to the sword and the lance.
But since their theology
Frowned on biology
The poor buggers hadn't a chance.

When the Popes had tired of sending Crusaders to fight the infidel enemy abroad, they turned to the infidel enemy within – the Cathars, or Albigensians in the Languedoc region of France.

In the first half of the thirteenth century, tens of thousands were killed in order to suppress the Cathar heresy. But what was so threatening about it? Well, the refusal to recognise a clerical hierarchy didn't go down well with the Pope. But they also had some controversial ideas about sex.

For Catholics, reproduction was king, but for Cathars it was a moral evil. Non-procreative sex, whether gay or straight, was better than making babies (the word 'bugger' comes from 'Bulgarian', as that's where the sect originated). This attitude can't have helped their survival prospects, even without the massacres.

KHAN YOU BELIEVE IT?

There was an old man from Mongolia
Whose deeds couldn't get much unholier.
The bloodthirsty bleeder
Was such a big breeder,
If he wanted yer babies, he stole yer.

Genghis Khan's attitude to reproduction was in marked contrast to that of the Cathars. Genetic testing has revealed that 16 million men (0.5 per cent of the world's male population) share a single Y-chromosomal lineage, reckoned to be his.

While creating the largest land empire in history around the beginning of the thirteenth century, Genghis went in for a lot of conquering, killing, burning and pillaging, and it's unlikely all of his sexual conquests were consensual. Though he only married six times, his harem was huge.

On the plus side, the Mongols were relatively tolerant in religious terms. And the size of their empire opened up the Silk Road to trade again, linking China and Europe: Europe got porcelain and gunpowder, China got buttons and the Black Death.

GET CARTA

There once was an old Magna Carta,
Giving rights to the top social strata.
The folks at the bottom,
They still hadn't got 'em
For that was, back then, a non-starter.

Amid all the conquest and pillage, challenges to absolute monarchy had begun to emerge. In England in the thirteenth century, powerful families began flexing their muscles against the King. That led to the creation of a document that's been claimed as the foundation of everything from Habeas Corpus (the right not to be unjustly detained) to the American Bill of Rights.

In 1215, 25 rebellious barons forced King John to put his seal to an agreement accepting, among other things, that no 'freeman' could be punished except through the law. But there wasn't much in it for the serfs, who could still be bought and sold.

John agreed under duress, then went back on his word, so the fight raged on. But the charter became a blueprint for the idea that people have rights. And it still is.

OH BONDAGE, UP YOURS!

A revolting old peasant named Wat
Rose up to protest at his lot,
But was killed by the Mayor
(See below for when, where
Why and how Wat was finally got).

So wat (to labour the pun) about the workers? What strengthened their position in mid-14th century Europe was the Black Death, which created a labour shortage by killing half the population.

In England the lords tried to stop people travelling in search of better paid work by freezing wages and restricting movement. Then, in 1381, the imposition of an unpopular poll tax was the last straw. Wat Tyler led an army of revolting peasants, labourers and artisans in a march on London, where they made the 14-year-old King Richard agree to abolish serfdom.

But while Wat and the King were chatting, the Mayor of London stabbed Tyler, and the peasants' revolt was put down. The teen king promptly withdrew his promise and vowed to punish the peasants with 50 shades of bondage instead.

HOLY ORDERS

There was a young woman named Joan,
Who heard voices when all on her own,
So she dressed as a bloke
To fight England's yoke,
As ordered by God on the phone.

The peasants were revolting in France too, but there wasn't much solidarity, as the two countries were busy with the Hundred Years' War. Many lived and died knowing only perpetual conflict.

Among them was Joan of Arc. She was only 12 in 1424, when she started having visions of saints telling her to drive the English out of France. She convinced the King to listen, and when they told her to dress as a man and lead the charge, she did just that.

But when the English eventually caught her, she was tried for heresy – mostly it seems for continued cross-dressing. Joan protested in vain that God told her to do it, and it helped prevent sexual harassment by the prison guards. In 1431 she was burned at the stake, and a successful appeal in 1456 was little comfort to Joan's corpse – though it perhaps aided her immortal soul.

GUT-ER PRESS

The invention of moveable type
Has largely lived up to the hype,
But the first man to print
Was generally skint
So published his fair share of tripe.

Johannes Gutenberg, born in Mainz somewhere around 1400, is generally credited with the invention of moveable type. The Chinese had worked out how to do it 400 years earlier, but with so many characters no one could be arsed to make printing presses.

Gutenberg's press made it possible to print numerous copies of books or pamphlets quickly, but he was an entrepreneur, driven by profit – and often by the need to repay a debt.

After one failed business venture, Gutenberg borrowed money to print Bibles, which his wonder presses duly delivered in 1455. And he had a sideline printing dodgy indulgences, which were at the heart of Martin Luther's criticism of the Catholic Church (see p.46) – criticism that was also aired using Gutenberg's technology.

RENAISSANCE MAN

Leonardo, the Renaissance man
Did much more than most people can —
Art, music, botany,
Faults? There were not-any
(Ignore that old novel by Dan).

Printing helped to spread the philosophy of the Renaissance, a cultural great leap forward. When Leonardo da Vinci began his apprenticeship as a painter in Florence in the 1460s, art, science and philosophy were all flourishing there. In between painting the 'Mona Lisa' and 'The Last Supper', Leonardo played a mean lyre, and studied botany and human anatomy. He also invented the helicopter and came up with the idea of solar power.

Any downsides? Well, he was accused of sodomy, but that's now legal in most places. And according to Dan Brown's *The Da Vinci Code*, he ran a secret society devoted to hiding the truth about Jesus's secret love children, but if so, Leonardo clearly did as good a job at the cover-up as at everything else he tried.

THE PAIN IN SPAIN

The friars of Spain's Inquisition
Were keen to encourage contrition,
So heretics, Jews
And Muslims could choose
Garrotting before their ignition.

After that dollop of enlightened modernism, you probably didn't expect a chapter on this – but then, no one expects the Spanish Inquisition! When the religiously tolerant Muslim caliphate of Al-Andalus (now Andalucia) was defeated by Catholic Spain in 1492, Jews and Muslims were given a choice – convert or leave.

But in case any of those wily heathens were just pretending to convert, Dominican friars led by Tomas de Torquemada took on the task of testing their faith. This soon became an excuse to torture anyone suspected of not being a good Catholic – heresy, witchcraft and sodomy were all capital crimes.

They may have been ruthless, sadistic, fanatical bigots, but if you repented, they would garrotte you before burning you. Unexpectedly considerate, really!

OH, COLUMBUS!

There was an old man named Columbus
Who was woken one night from his slumbers.
On deck in pyjamas
He saw the Bahamas
Not Asia – he'd messed up the numbers.

Christopher Columbus also left Spain in 1492, but voluntarily: he'd read about the riches of the East, and wanted a share. But the Silk Road was getting a bit inhospitable, so he went west in search of the Indies.

Following the theories of the Egyptian scientist Ptolemy, he believed the Earth was round. But he miscalculated its size, and failed to realise there was a lot of land and sea – the Americas and the Pacific Ocean – in the way.

One night Columbus was woken by a lookout who had spotted land – though he told everyone he'd seen it first. But Columbus insisted until his dying day that he had found the Indies – terms like 'West Indies' still reflect his mistaken belief.

NO QUARTER FROM CORTÉS

A Mexican named Moctezuma,
Who welcomed Cortés with good humour,
Thought Quetzlcoatl
Had come to do battle —
Or so went the colonists' rumour.

European adventurers soon flocked to the New World to carve out new conquests and make money. Among them was Hernán Cortés, who landed in Mexico with 600 mercenaries in 1518.

Despite massacring the first native peoples he encountered, Cortés was welcomed with open arms by the Aztec ruler, Moctezuma. According to the Spaniards, the Aztecs thought Cortés was their god Quetzcoatl, who was due for a reappearance – though that's disputed these days.

The Spanish moved into the palace and made themselves at home. Eventually they took Moctezuma hostage, and somewhere in the mêlée he was killed. The locals accused Cortés of murder, while the Spanish said his own people turned on him. Either way, no one's worshipping Cortés these days.

INCA-PACITATED

There once were some folk called the Incas,
Old farmers and builders and thinkers,
Whose world was to vanish
Soon after the Spanish
Brought guns and diseases, the stinkers.

If Cortés managed to take Mexico with a fairly small force, he had nothing on his cousin Francisco Pizarro, who headed south from Panama to find Peru. The Inca empire had only been going for about 90 years when Pizarro turned up with 13 followers in 1526, but it had mines, a sophisticated system of agriculture and a fantastic royal estate at Macchu Picchu.

Six years later Pizarro returned with 168 men (plus horses, armour, and guns). The Inca army was 80,000 strong, but most were reluctant conscripts. And the Emperor Atahualpa foolishly left his soldiers behind when he went for a chat with Pizarro, who had him kidnapped and killed.

But what did for the Incas were the diseases brought by the poxy invaders: smallpox wiped out more than half the population.

UNHEALTHY DIET

There was an old scholar named Martin,
Who decided he wanted no part in
The Diet of Worms,
Whose intransigent terms
Meant recanting what he'd put his heart in.

One day in 1517, German theologian Martin Luther posted his thoughts on a door – on his wall, if you like. He thought it was wrong for the church to raise funds by selling 'indulgences' – bits of paper that absolved people of their sins. Soon Martin's status update was getting a lot of 'likes'.

But these indulgences were a nice little earner for Vatican Inc, and its CEO, Pope Leo X, was not best pleased. So Martin was charged with heresy and summoned to the Diet of Worms.

This is not a reference to prison food – it was an assembly of the Holy Roman Empire held in the German town of Worms. Luther was told to recant and delete his posts. He refused, was excommunicated, and Leo unfriended him. The resulting split in the Church led to the schism between Protestants and Catholics.

THE EARTH MOVED

A Nick Copper-Knickers supporter
Said stuff that a chap didn't oughta.
Being heliocentric
Back then was eccentric
And so got him into hot water.

Scientists too ran the risk of being damned as heretics. Nicolaus Copernicus had managed to get away with saying the Earth went round the Sun back in 1543, so 70 years later Galileo Galilei probably thought he was on solid (if rapidly spinning) ground.

But whereas Copernicus presented his ideas as interesting-and-theoretically-useful-even-if-not-true (#justsayin'), Galileo went further. He tried to persuade the Church hierarchy that the Copernican model didn't conflict with the Bible.

The Inquisition gave Galileo a slap on the wrist. But when he then published a dialogue giving both sides of the argument, the Pope took umbrage. The book was banned and Galileo was found guilty of heresy and put under house arrest. Perhaps he shouldn't have called the pro-Pope character 'Simplicio'.

AXE THE MISSUS

There once was a man with six wives
Of varying sexual drives.
When each bore no heir
He would have an affair
And divorce them or else take their lives.

Henry VIII's beef with the Pope wasn't about whether the Earth went round the Sun, but whether he'd ever get a son, and what he was entitled to do with wives who failed to bear him one.

So when the Pope refused to grant him a divorce from his Spanish first wife, Catherine of Aragon, Henry made himself head of the Church in England in 1532. He then married his mistress, Anne Boleyn. But when she, like Catherine, could only produce a daughter, he cut off her head.

Henry's next wife, Jane Seymour, bore him a male heir, but died giving birth. And so it went on – divorced, beheaded, died, divorced, beheaded, survived. But the irony is, he'd had a son all along – an illegitimate boy borne by his mistress, Bessie Blount, years before.

FOREIGN FOOD

There once was a plant in Peru
Which old Inca farming folk grew.
The spread of this tuber
And baccy from Cuba
Meant Brits could eat chips and smoke too.

Back in the sixteenth century even a gourmand like Henry VIII might have rejected deep-fried, chipped potatoes as 'nasty foreign food'. Grown for centuries by the Incas, spuds were imported to Europe by the Spanish, and soon became a staple food.

As for tobacco, that was brought back from the Americas by the Spaniards, and rapidly turned into a big cash crop on slave plantations in the New World.

There was no health warning on the packs back then, but not everyone was keen on tobacco. In 1604, King James I denounced smoking as 'loathsome to the eye, hatefull to the nose, harmefull to the braine, dangerous to the Lungs, and resembling the horrible stigian smoke of the pit that is bottomless'. But rather than banning it, he taxed the stuff. Yeah, that'll stop it.

I AM A WEAKISH SPELLER

There was an old fellow named Will
Who wrote with rare humour and skill.
In sonnets and plays
He coined many a phrase,
But the sad fact is Will couldn't spill.

The Queen's English is filled with *household words* coined by, or popularised by, William Shakespeare. His works were responsible for a *sea change* in our language and literature that was to reach *all corners of the world*.

He wrote tragedies *to make your hair stand on end* and comedies to have you *in stitches*, and his sonnets were *such stuff as dreams are made on*. He knew that *brevity is the soul of wit*, though this was at times *honoured more in the breach than the observance* – the Bard could *lay it on with a trowel*.

Shakespeare coined all these phrases, and about 1,700 words. But his spelling would be given *short shrift* nowadays. And the title of this entry is an anagram. But *what's in a name?*

CRAPPY CHRISTMAS

There was an old general called Ollie
Who wasn't what I would call jolly.
He banned Christmas revels
As work of the devil's
Which fun-loving folk thought was folly.

Right, that's enough of that – sod off, Shakespeare and stop all this frivolous theatrical nonsense! Oh, and Christmas is cancelled! Oliver Cromwell was not actually the Grinch personified – the decision to ban Christmas festivities was taken during the English Civil War by the parliament, which was more into fasting than feasting. But Cromwell himself was pretty much of a puritan, and did ban sports and close down pubs.

With his execution of King Charles I in 1649, violent suppression of Catholic Ireland and the formation of the New Model Army, Cromwell polished his image as a hard man. But though he banned make-up for women, various soaps and cosmetics have been found in Cromwell's house. Perhaps they were unwanted Christmas presents.

A FRUITFUL DISCOVERY

There was an old fellow named Newton
Who was overly fond of disputin'.
It's good he was quizzical
As to things physical
(And that his garden had fruit in!)

Isaac Newton grew up under Cromwell, but was not a very good puritan – he later confessed to squirting water on a Sunday. Unusually for such anecdotes, the tale of Newton discovering gravity on seeing an apple fall from a tree appears to be true – or if it isn't, it was Newton himself who invented it.

Newton's 1687 work *Principia Mathematica* changed our understanding of how the natural world works. He also influenced enlightenment philosophers, who tried to extend the idea of a universe governed by rational laws to the political sphere.

But though Newton loved an argument with a fellow scientist (he had a long feud with Leibniz), he wasn't that interested in politics. He became an MP, but spoke only to say there was a bit of a draught, and could someone please close the window.

BY COOK OR BY CROOK

An explorer named Captain James Cook
Sailed off round the world for a look.
Now Britain could plunder
The riches Down Under
And lose the occasional crook.

Actually, this is a bit unfair to old Cooky. Like Newton, his interest was in science – in his case geography and astronomy – rather than imperial conquest. But as he was stargazing in the Pacific, the Navy told him to go off and find the great continent of Terra Australis that everyone was convinced must be down there.

After sailing around long enough to realise that Australia and New Zealand weren't part of a bigger land mass, Cook landed at Botany Bay in 1770 and claimed the land for Britain, which found it rather useful as a penal colony.

This wasn't great for the existing inhabitants. The settlers weren't all crims – many came for the gold rush – but they brought problems such as smallpox, alcohol and racism. The indigenous population dropped from at least 300,000 to just 60,000.

HONEST FELLER?

George Washington? Helluva guy,
They say that the man couldn't lie
'Who cut down the tree?'
Asked his pop. 'It was me.'
(You're in politics, George – at least try!)

You may have heard about how 6-year-old George, confronted by his father as to who might be responsible for the hatchet job on his cherry tree, famously replied 'I cannot tell a lie – I did it'. Ironically, the story was made up by Washington's biographer to make the first President of the United States look good.

Washington did have a pretty distinguished career even without such embellishment; he was commander of American forces in the War of Independence from 1775–83; he did a decent job of uniting the various troops from different colonies; and under GW the army was briefly racially mixed.

He also farmed cannabis, though only to get hemp for ropes. And as for honesty, Mr Goody-two-shoes borrowed two books from a New York library in 1789, and didn't return them.

TROUBLE BREWING

Americans living in Boston
Resented how much things were costin'.
They took loads of tea
Off the ships to the sea
Where the stuff was immediately tossed in.

The American Revolution began as a storm in a teacup. People in Britain's American colonies didn't like the way the Brits were using the tax on tea to raise money.

Since the colonists took no part in British elections, it flew in the face of the principle of 'No taxation without representation'. Protests at American ports in 1773 stopped tea being unloaded, and things came to a head in Boston when a crowd of people stormed the ships and chucked it in the sea.

The Brits were upset, because the tea should be put in the pot before the water, which must be freshly boiled. Two years later, America and Britain were at war, and in 1776 the US declared its independence. Now they drink lattes.

HALF-BAKED SUGGESTION

The dauphine Marie Antoinette
Heard French people had no baguette.
Saying 'Let them eat cake'
Was a foolish mistake,
For which the Queen paid with her tête.

While tea was making Americans boil, the French were rising up about the price of bread. But the rumour that Marie Antoinette, wife of King Louis XVI, said 'Let them eat cake' (well, brioche) was started by the political philosopher Jean-Jacques Rousseau.

The lower and middle classes were fed up about the amount of dough they had to cough up in taxes, while the cake-eating aristocracy scooped the cream. And enlightenment thinkers like Rousseau, who argued for a society based on reason, provided the yeast in the revolutionary ferment.

But French patissiers do have something to thank Marie Antoinette for. She may have lost her loaf during the Revolution, but she was widely credited with introducing the croissant to Paris from her native Vienna.

COURTING TROUBLE

There once was an old tennis court,
Where in place of the usual sport
They served revolution —
A new constitution
Won everyone's pledge of support.

Marie Antoinette's husband was used to winning, as an absolute monarch. But Louis XIV was broke, so in 1789 he created a limited democracy with blocs elected by a) the clergy, b) the nobles, and c) everybody else (well, male taxpayers over 25).

Louis soon realised 'everybody else' added up to quite a lot, and tried to stop them meeting. Locked out of the assembly, they went to a tennis court where they served up a declaration paving the way for a new constitution. The King batted it back, but the ball was in the revolutionaries' court now.

If the tennis court oath was the first set, the storming of the Bastille – the prison where the King kept his ammunition – was the second. And by 1792, when popular militias stormed the palace and took the King prisoner, it was game, set and match.

MAKE WAR NOT LOVE

Frenchman Napoleon Bonaparte
And his wife Josephine having grown apart,
On the eve of a fight
He said 'Jo — not tonight.
I think we should sleep on our own-apart.'

After autocratic monarchy and a few years of revolutionary terror under Robespierre, France clearly needed a megalomaniac emperor. Enter Napoleon Bonaparte. After taking power, the Corsican general conquered almost all of Europe, before being beaten by British and Prussian forces at Waterloo in 1815.

Napoleon and Josephine did grow apart – they divorced and then remarried in 1810 – but there is no evidence he ever said 'Not Tonight, Josephine' on the eve of battle. It was probably a story put about by his enemies, like the myth that Napoleon was short.

In fact, it's thought he was about 5ft 6in (168cm), above average for a Frenchman of the time. But that was 5ft 2 in French inches, hence the confusion. And perhaps that also explains why Napoleon was so keen to introduce the metric system!

PLANTATION NATION

There once was a prominent Haitian
Who campaigned for e-mancipation,
Helped slaves to rebel,
Gave the slave-owners hell
And set up a sovereign nation.

Napoleon's rule was in many ways a backward step. Brutal as the revolutionary idealists may have been, they did introduce democracy, and even abolished slavery in French colonies – only for Bonaparte to bring it back.

But in Haiti, revolutionary fervour had already taken hold, as a series of slave revolts in 1791 turned into a liberation war led by a freed slave called Toussaint L'Ouverture. In 1801 he wrote a friendly letter to Napoleon 'From the leader of the blacks to the leader of the whites', urging him to reconsider the slavery issue.

Napoleon's response was to send an army, which was beaten by the Haitian rebel forces. But it was too late for Toussaint. Captured and imprisoned in France, he died of pneumonia in 1803 – eight months before Haiti won its independence.

CREAM OF CARACAS

There was an old man of Caracas
Who engaged Spanish troops in a fracas.
Conspiracists think
Someone poisoned his drink
(Old Chávez was one of their backers).

Newly independent Haiti was small, but it was not without influence. In 1816, Haiti financed and provided troops for Simon Bolivar's War of Independence in Spanish-occupied South America – on condition he abolished slavery there.

When Bolivar died in 1830, doctors put it down to tuberculosis. But more recent research has suggested his symptoms were consistent with arsenic poisoning. Everyone loves a good conspiracy story, not least the late Venezuelan president Hugo Chávez. Almost 200 years later, he ordered a fresh autopsy on Bolivar's body. Alas, it revealed no signs of foul play.

Come to that, there's no evidence the CIA gave Chávez and a number of other left-leaning Latin American leaders cancer, as he's suggested.

MARY, MARY

There was a young woman named Mary
Whose lifestyle was seen as contrary.
An unmarried mum,
Her time has now come
But many men then found her scary.

Amid all this liberation, a few voices began to be raised for women's rights. One belonged to Mary Wollstonecraft, whose *Vindication of the Rights of Women* (1792), laid out the principles of gender equality that paved the way for eventual women's suffrage.

But back then she was best known as that scandalous hussy who ran off to join the French Revolution, and had a child with a married man. After her death in childbirth, the father of her second child, William Godwin, wrote a memoir that shocked polite society, and may have made it harder for her work to be appreciated. Or maybe feminism scared the male establishment.

The daughter whose birth proved fatal was Mary Shelley, who grew up to write the properly scary *Frankenstein*. So Frankenstein's creator's creator was inadvertently killed by her own creation.

ROCKET MAN

There was an old man of the Tyne
Who pioneered railway design.
He won at Rainhill,
But saw his train kill
A man who strayed on to the line.

As well as all these political revolutions, there was an industrial revolution going on, and that's how we got trains. Railway pioneer George Stephenson, for example, was a Newcastle-born miner whose interest in rail started with shifting coal, not people.

But he then got involved in constructing the Liverpool to Manchester railway, one of the first passenger lines. And when they held trials at Rainhill in 1829 to choose an engine for the new line, Stephenson's *Rocket* won.

Sadly, at the inauguration of the line a Liverpool MP named William Huskisson stepped off one of the only two passenger trains operating in the world, and was hit by the other one – the *Rocket* – coming in the opposite direction. What were the chances of that?

TOLPUDDLE MUDDLE

There once were six Tolpuddle martyrs
Who were punished by County Court tartars
(Though martyrdom proper
Means facing the chopper —
Or anyway dying, for starters!)

From a man who was killed while being transported, to six others who were transported, but not killed. Don't get me wrong, I'm not saying they should have hanged, it's just that the word 'martyr' tends to be used for someone who dies for their religious beliefs.

But these six farm labourers from Dorset in southwest England were not executed in 1832, they were merely transported to Australia, which allowed a successful campaign led by the Chartist political reformers to bring them back.

The crime of these men, who have since been adopted as heroic pioneers of trade unionism, was swearing an oath to form a friendly society, to protest against their wages being cut from nine shillings a week to six. I know swearing's bad, but couldn't they just have put a shilling each in the effing swearbox?

THE WAR FOR DRUGS

A Chinese official named Lin
Thought trading in drugs was a sin
So the Brits fought two wars
In the dubious cause
Of the right to ship opium in.

In the nineteenth century China's self-sufficiency and isolation caused two problems for Britain: industrial production demanded new markets, and Brits required tea. All the tea in China.

But the Chinese weren't interested in trade, so the East India Company came up with the bright idea of flogging the Chinese opium, a drug so addictive that it rapidly created demand where none had existed. To combat this, Lin Zexu was made China's drug czar in 1838, and promptly threw all the opium in the sea.

Unfortunately, the drug traffickers' overall boss was a super-pusher called Britain, who promptly sent in gunboats and offered a deal China couldn't refuse – including the surrender of Hong Kong on a long lease. So in the first battle in what has since been called the 'War on Drugs', drugs won hands down.

FULL MARX

There was an old man with a beard
Who said 'It is just as I feared –
This mode of production
Entails self-destruction
But hasn't as yet disappeared'.

Karl Marx understood a lot about how capitalism was changing the world. But he couldn't work out why the masses didn't overthrow their capitalist oppressors. Ultimately, he believed the bourgeoisie was producing 'the seeds of its own destruction'.

After the failure of the revolts of 1848 in Europe, Marx ended up in Britain, which as the most industrialised nation he saw as the best hope for revolution. The penniless émigré spent his time writing and trying to keep the debt collectors from the door.

In this he was helped by his pal Friedrich Engels, whose family owned some cotton mills in Manchester. Managing them gave Engels an insight into capitalist production, but also involved hanging out with the bourgeoisie in the Cheshire Hunt – quite literally running with the Herr and hunting with the hounds.

PATRIOT GAMES

Garibaldi made Italy one
With a small bunch of mates and a gun,
While Otto von Bismarck,
A German, made his mark,
Well armed, but perhaps with less fun.

Giuseppe Garibaldi and Otto von Bismarck, who helped unite Italy and Germany in 1860 and 1870, reacted very differently to the 1848 revolutions. Garibaldi joined the uprising in Rome, hoping to oust the foreign powers that had carved up Italy; while Prussian aristocrat Bismarck offered his support to protect King Frederick William from the rabble.

Born in Nice, Garibaldi fought the Bourbon rulers but hobnobbed with King Victor Emmanuel. So he basically spent his time collecting the names of biscuits yet to be invented. Bismarck, on the other hand, gave his name to a battleship and the state capital of North Dakota, but no biscuits. Seventy years later the two countries were fascist buddies. A product of national political immaturity – or just the way the cookie crumbles?

NURSING A GRIEVANCE

There once was a nurse from Jamaica,
A regular mover and shaker.
She went to a camp
Where a lass with a lamp
Refused for some reason to take 'er.

By the 1850s, when Britain, France and Russia were fighting the Crimean War, people were realising that decent hygiene and nutrition kept soldiers alive. Well-connected Florence Nightingale got herself despatched with a team of nurses to Turkey.

But experienced Jamaican nurse Mary Seacole was turned down by the War Office in London, so she headed for Turkey under her own steam. She offered her help to Florence, but was rejected again, so she set up her own private operation.

It may have been racism, or perhaps Flo didn't want anyone cramping her style. Upright Nightingale disapproved of Seacole allowing her patients to drink, and accused her rival of keeping a brothel. I wonder which approach was more therapeutic …

FREE THINKER?

We're told it was Honest Abe's bravery
Ended the practice of slavery.
But some of the thinkin'
Of Abraham Lincoln
Appears to us now quite unsavoury.

US President Abraham Lincoln has gone down in history as the man who fought the Civil War to free the slaves. But as a politician, the views he expressed when appealing to white voters were not quite so progressive.

Lincoln often said he had been anti-slavery for as long as he could remember. But it was not until halfway through the Civil War, when the North needed to recruit African-American soldiers, that he issued his 1863 Emancipation Proclamation.

In 1858 he said that white people were superior to black people, and that the two races couldn't live together as equals, adding 'While they do remain together there must be a position of superior and inferior, and I am in favour of having the superior position assigned to the white race.' Lucky for racially superior Abe, we judge a man by his deeds, not his words!

TWO TRIBES

Old Sitting Bull, with Crazy Horse
Made quite a formidable force.
They managed to muster
The troops to beat Custer
But lost in the long run, of course.

While the slaves were being emancipated, the indigenous population in America was being decimated. As white settlers expanded the land under their control, often at the barrel of a gun, the Native Americans were forced into reservations.

But when General George Custer and his men found gold in the Great Sioux Reservation, it meant war. At the Battle of Little Big Horn in 1876, inspired by Sitting Bull's vision of a big defeat for their enemies, the Lakota and the Cheyenne attacked the US 7th Cavalry, killing Custer and several hundred men.

Within a few years, though, their forces had been broken up. Crazy Horse, the hero of Little Big Horn, was killed, and Sitting Bull ended up in Buffalo Bill Cody's Wild West Show, where he spent the rest of his days cursing tourists under his breath.

HOME RULER PLAYS AWAY

Irishman Charlie Parnell
Fought for Home Rule for a spell,
Till Kitty's divorce
Rather blew things off course –
His future, and Ireland's as well.

It is, of course, most unfair to distil the history of Irish resistance to British oppression into one man's marital problems – but what do you expect from a limerick book?

Charles Stewart Parnell, MP sought the break-up of the union between England and Ireland – seen by most Irish as a forced marriage. But being cited in Kitty O'Shea's divorce proceedings in 1889 destroyed his credibility in Catholic Ireland.

So instead he achieved the break-up of her marriage, of his own party and of the Liberal Party, which split over Home Rule. And the break-up of Britain and Ireland 30 years later was accompanied by a break-up between north and south. But at least the Republic of Ireland did eventually legalise divorce. In 1995.

ADAM AND EVOLUTION

Ideas of evolving humanity
Were frowned upon by Christianity.
Charles Darwin baboons
Soon appeared in cartoons
Lampooning the loony's insanity.

Creationists maintain God created the fossil record to tempt us into doubting Him. It certainly worked on Charles Darwin. Studies of South American fossils, as well as variations in finches, led him to the theory of evolution through natural selection set out in 1859 in *On the Origin of Species*.

Darwin held off going into the implications for humans initially, but other scientists such as T. H. Huxley weighed in. The evolutionists were roundly mocked and caricatured for suggesting that we descended from apes, rather than Adam and Eve.

In a debate Bishop Sam Wilberforce asked Huxley whether he was related to a monkey on his mother's or his father's side. But a few years ago, the Church of England issued an apology to Darwin – a sign of how even churches can evolve.

WHEN I GET THAT FEELIN' . . .

There was an old shrink from Vienna
Who reckoned both women and men're
Repressing true feeling,
Need sexual healing
(I think that's the general tenor).

If Darwin angered our nineteenth-century forebears by telling them of their animal ancestry, Sigmund Freud had another shock in store. He informed the respectable citizens of turn-of-the-century Vienna that men were in love with their mothers and wanted to kill their fathers, while the women had penis envy.

Among the things we owe to Freud are: the idea of the unconscious, repression of traumatic events; the Oedipus complex; the interpretation of dreams; subliminal (nipple) thoughts; transference; and of course the Freudian penis – I mean slip.

He believed our hang-ups are caused by anxiety about sex. A smoker, he thought all addictions were a substitute for onanism, and would apparently have agreed with Marvin Gaye's 'Sexual Healing': 'Please don't procrastinate, it's not good to masturbate'.

IT'S ALL RELATIVE

A patent official in Bern
Thought physicists had much to learn.
'Mein Gott!' he declared
'E's M times C squared
And space-time can slow down and turn'.

Albert Einstein was not just relatively bright. He did fail his college entrance exam, and went to work in the Bern patent office. But by 1905, aged 26, he'd completely rewritten our understanding of the world and the universe.

His most famous equation revealed the massive amount of energy stored in every atom, paving the way for nuclear fission. His special Theory of Relativity proved that time and space were not separate things, but part of a continuum. And his general Theory of Relativity showed how space-time could slow down, and could be bent by the pull of large objects. Are you with me so far? Luckily, Einstein came up with a handy analogy: 'When a man sits with a pretty girl for an hour, it seems like a minute. But let him sit on a hot stove for a minute and it's longer than any hour. That's relativity'.

THE WRIGHT STUFF

There once were two brothers named Wright
Who soared to a new dizzy height.
Though journalists laughed,
Their preposterous craft
Established manned aerial flight.

Wilbur and Orville Wright, two brothers who ran a bike-repair shop in Ohio, must have stood out among the ranks of gentleman scientists and amateur adventurers who built and flew the early flying machines of the early twentieth 20th century.

Their secrecy led the French to dismiss them as 'bluffeurs', while US newspapers asked whether they were 'fliers or liars'. But as businessmen, they weren't giving their plans away for free.

In November and December 1904, they managed a series of flights of over five minutes above a field in Ohio. But when journalists showed up, they refused to repeat the feat. Knowing they had the technology sorted, they held out for a firm contract before taking their Kittyhawk plane up again. After all, you don't get to take your bike home till you've paid for the repair.

HISTORY IS BUNK II

Car pioneer Henry Ford
Made a vehicle folks could afford.
A great automator,
But many years later
Surpassed by the Honda Accord.

'History is more or less bunk', Henry Ford said: 'The only history that is worth a tinker's damn is the history we make today.' But he made his own contribution to history, as well as to bunk.

Ford didn't invent the motor car, but he revolutionised its manufacture, pioneering the production line with his 1908 Model T. For a long time Ford Motor Company led the way, though it was eventually overtaken at the end of the century by Japanese carmakers such as Honda, who copied his formula and did it better.

Would he have cared? Perhaps not – Ford's racism was mainly directed at Jews. He used some of his wealth to publish anti-semitic material such as the notorious fake *The Protocols of the Elders of Zion*. Which was indeed history of the bunk school.

IT'TH UNTHINKABLE!

There was an old ship, the Titanic,
That was not only big but gigannic,
So who woulda thunk
That it'd get sunk
By an iceberg out in the Atlannic.

Part of the reason the sinking of the *Titanic* on her maiden voyage in 1912 still resonates is because she was billed as unsinkable. As such she has gone down (as it were) in history as a metaphor for human hubris – a modern-day version of the Greek legend of Icarus, who flew too close to the sun and landed with a bump.

In fact, the claim wasn't seriously made, though some of the pre-publicity did use formulations such as 'designed to be unsinkable' that left a little legal wriggle-room.

But when the vice president of the White Star Line received a call to say the ship was in trouble – and had already taken 1,500 people to a watery grave – he replied: 'We place absolute confidence in the *Titanic*. We believe the boat is unsinkable.' That didn't sink his career, though – he was later promoted.

UPPING THE ANTE

There was an equestrian course
Where Emily jumped the King's horse.
She sought Votes for Women
And tried to drag him in,
While men deplored such use of force.

In Britain the Suffragettes were a movement of women who were fed up with the lack of progress of more mainstream suffragist campaigning, and resorted to direct action – chaining themselves to railings, smashing windows and stuff like that. Many were imprisoned, went on hunger strike and got force-fed.

Things came to a head in 1913, when Emily Davison ran in front of King George V's horse at Epsom with a 'Votes for Women' banner, and was knocked down and killed. Some say she couldn't actually have picked the King's horse out of the runners and riders as they thundered past – so what were the odds on that?

Male politicians condemned violent tactics, but eventually passed a Women's Suffrage bill five years later, after presiding over the deaths of 15 million people in the First World War.

SNACK ATTACK

Three shots outside Schiller's food store
And Franz Ferdinand was no more.
But was there a sandwich
Clutched tight in the hand which
Had triggered an all-out world war?

The assassination of the Austrian Archduke Franz Ferdinand in Sarajevo was the spark that lit the fuse of the First World War. Though perhaps another baking metaphor might be more apt, because there is some debate over the role a sandwich played in the events of that fateful day in July 1914.

After Bosnian Serb plotters missed the Archduke's motorcade with a grenade, some of them – so the story goes – nipped off to Schiller's Deli for a BLT. One, Gavrilo Princip, was standing outside eating his sarnie when the royal motorcade passed by. Princip duly drew his gun and shot the Archduke three times.

But though the Earl of Sandwich had invented the snack in 1760, there's no evidence it had reached Sarajevo by 1914. It's more likely Princip was eating a burek – like a Bosnian Cornish pasty.

MONK-Y BUSINESS

There was a mad monk named Rasputin
Whose allies were quite highfalutin',
But the elderly mystic
Made some go ballistic
Which caused his eventual shootin'.

Grigori Rasputin had the ear of the Russian Queen — and possibly other parts, so the Russians said. The charismatic Russian mystic told the Tsarina Alexandra to keep the doctors away from her son, and the boy's haemophilia appeared to improve (this may say more about the standards of medical care than Rasputin's gifts).

He told followers that the path to redemption was to give in to temptation — something he did as often as possible, according to the records of the secret policemen sent to spy on him.

But in 1916 there were fears he was using his influence over the Tsarina to try and get Russia out of the war. The old healer was poisoned then shot and — when that didn't work — clubbed to death by a group of young Russian nobles. But rumours of British Secret Service involvement also refuse to die.

REVOLTING RUSSIANS

There was an old man named Kerensky
Who made Russia's outside defence key
The workers rebelled
And Kerensky was felled.
He should have made their recompense key.

I know what you're thinking here – the Russian Revolution's about Lenin, not Kerensky. But do you mean the October Revolution (which happened in November) or the February Revolution (which took place in March)?

The second (or first) overthrew the Tsar, replacing him with a provisional government under Alexander Kerensky, who kept the war going. He was then kicked out by Lenin and the Bolsheviks, who promised hungry and war-weary Russians not just a new Communist utopia, but also bread and peace.

Oddly enough, the two men came from the same town, Simbirsk, where Kerensky's dad was Lenin's headmaster. It was subsequently renamed Ulyanovsk after Vladimir Ilyich Ulyanov – aka Lenin. Poor Kerensky.

THE LATE DICTATOR

There was an Italian dictator
Who swore none had ever been greater –
He'd cracked down on crime,
And made trains run on time
But the truth will out sooner or later.

Soon after the world's first Communist leader, we got the first fascist – Mussolini. Musso tends to get off lightly compared to Hitler, because he was less murderous and anti-Semitic. He was a tough guy, we hear, but he did clamp down on organised crime – and 'At least he made the trains run on time'.

But, while it's true that *Il Duce* jailed lots of Mafia bosses, contemporary accounts seem to agree that a) the trains improved a bit due to a reorganisation just before he took power in 1922, and b) actually, they were still pretty crap.

But being a dictator's great – you want everyone to believe something, you just tell them to. Except they don't, and when you finally lose power your beloved subjects hang you upside down from a meat hook and spit on you.

THE FAMILY BUSINESS

The Mafia boss Al Capone
Found rivals were accident-prone.
He covered his tracks,
But failed to pay tax
So was in the end overthrown.

Mussolini's crackdown on the Mob in Sicily helped it to emerge as a major force in the US, just as the prohibition of alcohol in 1920 was creating a massive illegal industry with huge profits.

Al Capone was born in Brooklyn to Italian parents, and by the age of 22 had control of a thriving Chicago bootlegging empire. His model for expansion consisted of killing his rivals and taking their business, while buying off the cops so he never got caught.

Capone saw himself as a good capitalist, and by 1929 he was raking in about $100 million from his various rackets. So the Feds decided to do him for tax evasion. Capone spent the 1930s in prison, and by his release prohibition had ended and his power had waned. And he had syphilis. If only he'd paid income tax!

BARE MARKET

There once was a stock market bubble
*That burst, leaving **Wall Street** in trouble.*
*A **US** recession*
Sparked global depression
As shares were sold off at the double.

Al Capone was far from the only businessman on the make in the 1920s. As shares soared everybody wanted in on the act, and all kinds of clever financial products were created to allow investors to make money out of money, rather than from making stuff.

In 1929 Irving Fisher, who's been called the first celebrity economist, said confidently that the stock market seemed to have reached 'A permanently high plateau'. However, this plateau turned out to be a bubble, and shortly afterwards it burst, causing a worldwide depression in which millions lost their jobs.

Luckily, humans are wise creatures, and we swore thereafter not to be so foolish as to ever let such a thing happen again, so the markets lived happily ever after. (See p.125.)

A LACK IN THE SACK?

Hitler, the Number One Nazi
In youth, we are told, was quite artsy.
So what made him later
A fascist dictator?
He lacked one significant part, see.

The Depression that followed the Wall Street Crash helped pave the way for the Nazis' rise to power in 1933. But how important was Hitler's character in making Nazi Germany the most inhumane mass-murdering regime in modern history, directly responsible for the deaths of six million Jews and millions of others?

Hitler's early life was one of setbacks and rejections: he was turned down by the Academy of Fine Arts in Vienna; as a soldier he felt humiliated by Germany's defeat in the First World War.

He was also known to have been wounded in the groin during the War, and a Soviet autopsy report found that he did, as had long been rumoured, only have one ball. Could this crucial lack in the sack have explained everything that came afterwards? No, sorry. You want a proper explanation? Go read a proper history book.

GORI STORY

There was an old fellow from Gori
Who basked in the Power and Glory,
As number one red.
But once he was dead,
Well, that was a different story.

Joseph Stalin had balls. But he was a nasty piece of work too. Born in Gori, Georgia, he chose the name Stalin or 'man of steel', and ruled the Soviet Union (USSR) with an iron fist. His treatment of opponents and former comrades was, well, gory.

During his 30-year rule, they were rounded up in gulags, or forced to confess to betraying the Revolution, then executed, until the old autocratic tsars almost started to seem liberal.

Stalin probably imagined dying fighting for the Revolution. Instead he had a stroke in 1952, and was found on his bedroom floor in urine-stained pyjamas. His infamous secret police chief, Lavrentiy Beria, reportedly ranted at Stalin as he lay unconscious, then started kissing his hand when he came to – only to spit on him when he passed out again. Even steel corrodes in the end.

WINNIE'S WINNING WAY

Churchill the great wartime leader
An artist, a writer and reader,
Made excellent speeches
Like 'fight on the beaches'
But drunk, he was quite a rude bleeder.

Winston Churchill was best known for his cigars – and speeches. Oratory such as, 'We shall fight them on the beaches', and 'I have nothing to offer but blood, toil, tears and sweat', delivered over the radio during the 1939–45 war, is credited with helping Britain to fight on while the Allies waited for America to join in.

Of course, making speeches like that, you'd need to wet your whistle. And wet it he did. In later life, he drank a bottle of champagne with lunch and another with his evening meal.

Accosted once by a woman MP, who said: 'Winston, you are drunk, and what's more you are disgustingly drunk!' he reportedly replied: 'My dear, you are ugly, and what's more you are disgustingly ugly. But tomorrow I shall be sober and you will still be disgustingly ugly.'

GONE FISSION

When scientists made atoms fissile
They didn't at first think 'With this I'll
Lay waste half the earth'.
But that was the birth
Of the A-bomb and nuclear missile.

Fat Man and Little Boy may sound like 80s rappers, but they were in fact the code names of the atomic bombs dropped on Hiroshima and Nagasaki in July 1945. These two harmless-sounding chappies killed 150,000–200,000 people, ended the war in Asia and introduced the world to the horrors of nuclear fallout.

The bomb was made possible by the discovery of uranium fission in 1939. Einstein, by then a refugee from the Nazis, feared the Germans might develop a nuclear bomb and helped persuade President Roosevelt that the US had to do it first. The Germans never did get the bomb, and Einstein later regretted his role.

After the war a growing nuclear club poured money into global dick-swinging, and now every autocratic regime wants centrifuges and Dong missiles. For the moment we're still here.

RELAX, DON'T DO IT

There was an old fellow named Gandhi
Whose self-control came in quite handy.
He frequently kipped
Next to women who'd stripped
And apparently didn't get randy.

Amid the violence of the Second World War, Mahatma Gandhi showed how non-violent resistance can bring about change, campaigning to peacefully end British rule in India.

Sadly, he failed to prevent partition along religious lines into India and Pakistan in 1947, or the accompanying violence in which hundreds of thousands died. Gandhi himself was assassinated by a Hindu nationalist who saw him as soft on Muslims.

Gandhi's political championing of the poor and oppressed went along with a spiritual world-view that venerated non-violence, poverty and chastity. To strengthen his resolve in the latter department, he regularly slept naked with young women, claiming that his self-control was such that he was able to do so without anything happening. It must have been hard.

ZION OF THE TIMES

There was a new state for the Jews
Which God was required to choose.
But Arab folks there
Didn't think it was fair
Which explains why it's still in the news.

And the Lord said unto Abraham: 'I will give unto you … all the land of Canaan, for an everlasting possession'. And many long years later the Lord Balfour said that the Brittites viewed with favour a national home for the Jewish people in Palestine.

But many among the Palestinites that did dwell in that land did protest. Some did smite the Israelites, and the Brittites. And some Israelites did smite the Palestinites and the Brittites for getting in the way. So the Brittites did go.

And in 1947 the peoples of the world decreed that the land should be divided into the land of Palestine and the land of Israel, but the smiting did continue. And some did say maybe people could live together and forget to whom God promised what. But they went unheard amid the smiting.

A WIDELY-RED MAN

There was an old chap, Mao Zedong,
Who commanded a March that was Long,
Wrote a Book that was Red
From the stuff that he said
And insisted that sex kept him strong.

Chairman Mao led the People's Republic of China from its foundation in 1949 to his death in 1976. His Little Red Book was a must-have in the West, and a must-have-or-else in China.

Depending on your point of view, he, a) brought China into the modern era, b) presided over the deaths of millions through purges and famine, c) transformed a feudal, foot-binding society into one with considerable equality and women's rights, d) fostered terror and backwardness through the cultural revolution's campaign against intellectuals, or e) all of the above.

His physician claimed Mao's view of women's rights eventually extended to the universal right to sleep with the Great Helmsman himself, who had decided that the Taoists were right, and sex could prolong life by mixing a little yin into a chap's yang.

THE HUMAN ENIGMA

IT pioneer Alan Turing,
Whose legacy's been quite enduring,
Helped crack the enigma
But suffered a stigma —
His gayness subjected to 'curing'.

British mathematician Alan Turing may have had more effect on the course of the post-war world than many. As early as 1936, he created the Turing machine, a hypothetical computer that paved the way for later, actual devices.

During the Second World War he turned his talents to cracking the German Navy's codes, as a leading member of the team of British code breakers at Bletchley Park. His 'bombe' machine was able to find the settings for the Nazis' Enigma machine, and it is estimated that this work may have shortened the war by two to three years.

But Turing was gay, and in the 1950s homosexuality was illegal in most countries, including the UK. Convicted of gross indecency with another man, he avoided prison by agreeing to chemical castration, to 'cure' him of his sexuality. Yes, they tried to reprogramme the father of programming. Two years later he died of cyanide poisoning. The inquest ruled it was suicide.

GET UP, SIT DOWN

A woman in South Alabama
Was arrested and chucked in the slammer
For causing a fuss
With her seat on a bus,
But the world was improved by this clamour.

Almost 100 years after the abolition of slavery, race discrimination was still the law in much of the southern US. African-Americans were deprived of the vote by restrictive registration practices, and schools, transport, restaurants and government facilities were segregated.

One day in 1955, in Alabama, Rosa Parks refused to move and give up her seat for a white passenger: she stood up for her rights by sitting down. A year-long walk-to-work bus boycott hit the bus company's profits so hard the law was changed.

The Civil Rights Act of 1964 ended segregation, but only after a lot more walking. In 1963 some 300,000 people marched on Washington, where Martin Luther King recounted his dream – so he was even standing up for his rights when lying down!

PARTY WALL

There was a big wall in Berlin
That was built to keep East Germans in,
While the state crushed subversion
Through fear and coercion
And stored suspect smells in a tin.

Over in Europe new Cold War barriers were going up. The East German Government called the wall it built through the middle of Berlin one night in 1961, the 'Anti-Fascist Protection Rampart': 'Protection' meaning shooting anyone who tried to climb over it.

The name was designed to suggest that West Germany had not been properly de-Nazified. This was not unfounded. But the East German Secret Police, the Stasi, were doing a pretty good job of picking up Hitler's mantle of anal totalitarianism.

Information about suspected subversives was obsessively recorded, including an archive of counter-revolutionary smells stored in jars. This was no help in 1989, when breaches elsewhere in the Iron Curtain led Berliners to break down the wall before the Government got even a whiff of the coming transformation.

THE ASCENT OF MAN

There was a young fellow named Yuri,
The Russians contrived to ensure 'e
Was first in the race
To get into space,
Provoking American fury.

The Cold War was initially played out largely through the Arms Race. But once the US and the USSR both had the bomb they needed a new race. So they invented the Space Race.

And to everyone's surprise, Russia won round one, sending Yuri Gagarin into space on 12 April 1961. After a quick orbit round the Earth, Gagarin landed. NASA technicians got a rocket from the politicians for not getting there first, but the Russians were over the moon, and milked his achievement for all it was worth.

The first man in space sadly died in a plane crash in 1968. But he spent the intervening seven years enjoying the trappings of international celebrity to the full – speaking tours, alcohol-fuelled receptions, women throwing themselves at him, and even an open-top motorcade through Manchester in the rain!

A CLOSE SHAVE

There was an old man named Fidel
Whom agents attempted to fell.
Their schemes were quite weird,
Like spiking his beard
And cigars that would blow him to hell.

The Cold War peaked with the Cuba Missile Crisis of 1962, when nuclear war was narrowly averted over the presence of Soviet missiles in what the US saw as its backyard.

Fidel Castro had been in power in Cuba for three years by then, and the CIA had already tried to get rid of him in numerous ways. Over the succeeding decades, they kept trying but he always seemed to emerge unhurt, like a cartoon baddy.

A few years ago, Castro's former bodyguard claimed there had been 638 plots to kill this thorn in Uncle Sam's backside. They included poison pen-syringes, bombs hidden in shells when he went diving, and exploding cigars. The CIA even considered a depilatory cream to make his beard fall out! Castro's beard stayed with him till the end, but he gave up smoking in 1985.

VIEW TO A KILL

The murder of President Kennedy
Made many folks loudly ask when 'ad 'e
Deserved such a fate?
And sparked much debate
As to who was behind this obscenity.

John F. Kennedy, US President at the time of the Cuban crisis, wasn't so lucky when it came to assassinations. Okay, he was only assassinated once, but that's all it takes.

JFK was not a well man – he got terrible headaches if he went without sex for three days. And he may have made a few enemies. But Kennedy was killed in 1963 by Lee Harvey Oswald in the book depository with a rifle. Not Colonel Mustard in the Billiard Room with the Lead Piping, whatever you may have read on the Internet.

Unless, of course, there was a second shooter on the grassy knoll. Working for the CIA. Or the KGB. Or the Cubans. Or the Mafia? And Oswald was killed by Jack Ruby, a nightclub operator with links to organised crime. In a police station. So, nothing suspicious there.

HAILE WELL-SPOKEN

The Emperor of Ethiopia
Blamed war on a racist myopia.
If people were equal
He reckoned the sequel
Would be one big peaceful utopia.

I admit my knowledge of Haile Selassie's speech to the United Nations in October 1963 – just six weeks before Kennedy's assassination – comes from Bob Marley, who set it to music in the song 'War'. But it bears repeating: 'Until the philosophy, that holds one race superior and another inferior, is finally and permanently discredited and abandoned, everywhere is war'.

In the midst of decolonisation in Africa and the civil rights movement in the US, this powerful ant-racist message of tolerance helps to explain why the Ethiopian Emperor became a religious figure to Rastafarians. That and the fact he'd been around virtually since biblical times – well, since the 1930s anyway.

But having listened to the original speech in Amharic, I say the UN should set all its debates to a reggae backing track.

PULLING APARTHEID APART

There was an old man named Mandela
Who's seen as a jolly good fella.
Though back in the day
They locked him away,
Today his approval rate's stellar.

Around this time, a young black South African activist visited Ethiopia for secret military training. Selassie gave him a gun. Nelson Mandela was leading armed resistance to the apartheid system, which divided South Africa's population along racial lines, with total segregation and with all power in white hands.

Mandela spent 27 years in prison, seen by the apartheid government and its allies as a terrorist; in the 1980s Conservative activists in Britain still sported 'Hang Nelson Mandela' badges.

What made Mandela remarkable was his dignity during his captivity, and the way he worked for unity and a non-violent transition to majority rule after his release. He was president from 1994–99, and in 2008 the US even took Mandela and his African National Congress off its list of terror organisations.

FLY ME TO THE MOON

There was an old fellow named Neil
Whose achievement was quite a big deal.
He stepped on the moon,
Although very soon
Some people denied it was real.

After Gagarin's flight, JFK promised the US would put a man on the moon before 1970. In July 1969, Apollo 11 took Neil Armstrong and Buzz Aldrin there and 500 million people watched on TV.

Knowing how big a deal this was for the US, conspiracists were quick to cast doubt. Sceptics pointed to the way the US flag seemed to flutter in a non-existent lunar breeze, as well as other evidence that the landing was filmed in a TV studio.

Okay, but as he walked on the moon, Neil Armstrong could be heard saying 'One small step for man, one giant leap for mankind'. Not 'for *a* man', which would have made much more sense – he fluffed his lines. At which point, the director of a staged landing would have shouted: 'Cut!'

LOSING AT DOMINOES

There was an old Uncle named Sam
Who sent lots of men to Vietnam
To prop up the dominoes,
But as every Commie knows
Ended up having to scram.

Cold War Europe was split into Communist East and capitalist West. But elsewhere for some reason, countries split into Communist North and Capitalist South. So after failing to kick the Commies out of North Korea in the 50s, the US tried again in North Vietnam in the 60s.

The US domino theory held that if you let one country go communist, like a line of dominoes, its neighbours will fall too. But the North Vietnamese turned out to be good at dominoes, and the American public really didn't want to play.

So in 1973 the US pulled out and Vietnam was free to pursue its own path. Which turned out to be a form of state capitalism – just like its neighbour, China. A domino effect?

OLD BUGGER

There was an old bugger called Nixon
Who tried any number of tricks on,
But just couldn't handle
The Watergate Scandal
Which journalists still get their kicks on.

President Richard Milhous Nixon's decision to bug the Watergate office complex in 1972 ensured that he is chiefly remembered as the only American President to resign.

And, of course, for services to journalism. The role played by Carl Bernstein and Bob Woodward of the *Washington Post* in exposing tricky Dicky's bugging of the Democratic Party HQ is something journalists rely on to show the importance of a free press whenever less glorious tabloid excesses such as phone-hacking are raised.

And since Watergate, the suffix '-gate' can be attached to any word to make it sound really, really bad; if you read about Limerickgate, you'll know I've done something like make up untrue historical anecdotes for the sake of a cheap rhyme.

AMIN TO SAY!

There was an old man from Uganda,
A pompous, bombastic grandstander.
Old President Idi
Ruled Scotland — or did 'e?
Well, so said Amin's propaganda.

From crap president to crap dictator. Others have been as ruthless in suppressing dissent, and disposing of political opponents, but Uganda's Idi Amin had the most absurd pretensions.

Amin seized power in 1971 – nine years after independence – with UK help. But he turned on the former colonial power, styling himself Lord of All the Beasts of the Earth and Fishes of the Seas and Conqueror of the British Empire in Africa in General and Uganda in Particular. He also took on the title of Last King of Scotland, pledging to free the Scots of the British yoke.

But while contemporaries such as Hastings Banda of Malawi, Mobutu Sese Seko of Zaire and Muammar Gaddafi in Libya were able to stick around for several decades, Amin was ousted after a mere eight years. Even the fishes saw through him.

KHOMEINI TIMES?

Khomeini, an old Ayatollah
(A word for a top Shia schollah)
Said 'I run Iran
'Cos I know my Koran
So the rest of you just better follah!'

Already in his late seventies when the pro-western Shah was overthrown in 1979, Ayatollah Ruhollah Khomeini outwitted a generation of leftist and liberal revolutionaries to turn Iran into an Islamic state.

Khomeini banned alcohol and non-religious music, stripped women of political and legal rights, and brought his interpretation of the Koran into every corner of life.

His writings do tend to focus on bodily fluids such as sweat and semen, but some of his views on sex have perhaps been distorted. I can't find anywhere Khomeini said it was okay to have sex with animals as long as you don't eat them. He simply said the meat of such animals is impure, and they should be burned – or if beasts of burden, sold in the next village. Quite tolerant, for him.

ARGY-BARGY

The Falklands, or else Las Malvinas
(For those to whom they're Argentina's)
Were used by Galtieri
When home life got hairy
As cover for his misdemeanours.

When Argentina invaded the Falkland Islands in 1982, public opinion in the UK was outraged. 'How dare they attack Scotland?' cried many an outraged Brit. Who knew they were actually in the South Atlantic, many thousands of miles away?

For Argentina it was a diversion from a severe economic crisis. Argentinian dictator General Leopoldo Galtieri decided the UK wasn't bothered about the Falklands, and dispatched a small force to take over the sparsely-populated archipelago.

But Prime Minister Margaret Thatcher was having none of this. Her naval task force took weeks to reach the islands, but swiftly dealt with a conscript Argentinian Army. It was a last hurrah for gunboat diplomacy, and a victory for geography. We now know where the Falklands are. But where's South Georgia?

BACK IN THE USSR

The policy known as glasnost
As Gorbachev found to his cost
Gave people a voice —
This expansion of choice
Being how the Cold War was then lost.

Glasnost and perestroika were not the twin mascots for the 1980 Moscow Olympics, they were policies introduced by Mikhail Gorbachev, who took over in 1985 – the first Soviet leader to be born after the 1917 revolution.

After years of stagnation, there was a need for economic restructuring (perestroika). But Gorbachev also believed that the USSR needed to allow more openness (glasnost). But open elections meant nationalists triumphed. People in many republics saw the USSR as a Russian empire, and by 1991 it had broken up.

Russia turned away from leaders ending in '-ev', like Khrushchev, Brezhnev and Gorbachev, longing for the days of the '-ins', Lenin and Stalin. Enter Yeltsin and Putin. Prime Minister Medvedev may need a name change to get a sniff of real power.

FINAL IRON CURTAIN

There was an old pair from Romania
Who suffered from megalomania,
None came to rescue
The leaders Ceausescu
When rifle rounds punctured their crania.

In 1988 Gorbachev abandoned the Brezhnev doctrine of keeping control of Eastern bloc countries for the Sinatra doctrine (do it your way, as in 'My Way'). So they all chose the Western way.

In Romania, 1989 got bloody. Nicolae and Elena Ceausescu had always relied less on the central committee, and more on the cult of personality, presiding over an impoverished police state in which every typewriter had to be registered.

Having begun building a palace that was to be the world's biggest, the Ceausescus had no intention of giving up without a fight, so they ordered troops to shoot any protesters who took to the streets. But the Army switched sides and the autocratic couple were summarily tried and executed by firing squad. Did they have any regrets? Too few to mention.

KILLER QUACK

The boss of the Bosnian Serbs
Was arrested one day in the 'burbs,
Pretending he wasnae a
Butcher of Bosnia,
Rather a healer with herbs.

The former Yugoslavia was hardest hit by ethnic violence as nationalism filled the vacuum left by communism.

A former psychologist, Bosnian Serb leader Karadzic was responsible for the 'ethnic cleansing' of Bosnian Muslims and Croats. He also shelled civilians in the besieged city Sarajevo, and ordered the massacre of 8,000 people at Srebrenica in July 1995. But when he was indicted for war crimes, the so-called 'Butcher of Bosnia' went on the run.

Karadzic was arrested in suburban Belgrade in 2008, where he had been working as an alternative health practitioner. He had tied his trademark shock of white hair up in a topknot and grown a long beard (a cunning disguise!), and was selling metal amulets as unconvincing as his justifications for genocide.

NET GAIN

A fellow named Tim Berners-Lee
First came up with HTTP.
The geeky celeb
Had invented the Web —
And he gave it to us lot for free.

As revolution swept Eastern Europe, a Brit in Switzerland was working on a revolutionary development. 'It discusses the problems of loss of information about complex evolving systems and derives a solution based on a distributed hypertext system,' wrote Tim Berners-Lee of his March 1989 proposal to improve the flow of information at the CERN nuclear research centre. Dull as it sounds, this is what allowed us all to use the Internet.

Even as the prophets of post-communism were pronouncing that only profit provided progress, Berners-Lee and his World Wide Web consortium decided it should be made available to everyone, with no patent protection or royalties. Allowing Google, Facebook, the porn industry *et al.* to make shedloads of money.

CHILEAN FEELS THE HEAT

There was a dictator from Chile
Who went quite unchallenged until 'e
Was nicked by police,
Securing release
When doctors declared he'd gone silly.

Augusto Pinochet's arrest in London in 1998 was, depending on your point of view, a triumphant rejection of dictatorial impunity or a savage blow against the inalienable right to seek medical treatment and retail therapy in London.

Having presided over mass arrests, torture, murder and disappearances in 1970s Chile, Pinochet left power in 1988 and was allowed to retire – until a Spanish judge had the bright idea of getting him arrested while in London. After 18 months of house arrest, Pinochet was sent back to Chile, having been deemed unfit to stand trial on grounds of ill health – specifically dementia.

Luckily, it was a special type of reversible dementia, and once back in Chile, he soon recovered. But by then, proceedings were under way against him there, halted only by his death in 2006.

NO WMD? WTF!

The West went to war against Saddam
Over weapons and whether 'e 'ad 'em.
The man from Tikrit
Was said to secrete
Certain arms though the UN forbade 'em.

Saddam Hussein faced a rather rougher form of justice. George Bush senior failed to get rid of him in the first Gulf War of 1990–91, so some 20 years later his son George W. took up the challenge.

Dubya had to act, of course, because: a) in 2001 some Arabs had attacked the World Trade Center and the Pentagon; b) Saddam was stockpiling chemical and biological weapons and trying to get nuclear arms; and c) he was a nasty dictator.

The problem was that a) was nothing to do with Iraq, and c) was just as much the case when Saddam was a US ally. So that left b). Evidence of Saddam's Weapons of Mass Destruction was duly found, war was waged, and he was overthrown and hanged in 2006. But the WMD were never found. Some troublemakers suggested the evidence was made up. OMG!

KOREA OPPORTUNITIES

There once were three Kims from Korea:
Two Leaders, the Great and the Dear,
And one rather lesser
Who's called the Successor,
But isn't succeeding, I fear.

One country that does have WMD is North Korea, whose leaders have created the kind of totalitarian dynasty Saddam dreamed of.

The old man and Great Leader, Kim Il-Sung, was officially designated Eternal President after his death, so he could continue to guide his son Kim Jong-Il from beyond the grave. The throne passed to Jong-Il's third son, Kim 'young 'un' Jong-Un in 2011 after his older brother tried to go to Disneyland on a forged passport.

So, how have the Kims held on to power for six decades? They haven't done all that well on basic stuff like making sure people have enough to eat. But they are very good at repressing political opponents, they have a huge army and their stadium displays are the envy of the world. Who needs Disneyland?

SPRING CLEANED

There was an old man of the Nile
With odious Laughing Cow smile.
As every dictator
Must sooner or later,
Old Mubarak had to stand trial.

Egyptian President Hosni Mubarak thought he had a pretty tight rein on the country too. But sometimes it just takes a small spark to ignite the tinder of discontent with dictatorship, and the whole thing goes up in flames.

When Tunisian street vendor Mohamed Bouazizi set himself on fire in January 2011, he lit the fuse of the Arab Spring, and Tunisian leader Zine El Abidine Ben Ali was the first to go.

Mubarak probably felt quite safe at first, even though people mocked him as the Laughing Cow — after a French brand of processed cheese. When crowds began to pack Tahrir Square night after night, they lost the fear. Eventually the Army came in and kicked him out — at which point he suddenly became too ill to stand trial. That old trick again!

OSAMA'S KARMA

The violent death of Osama
Was ordered by Barack Obama.
Some say of the leader
Behind al-Qaeda,
His dogma was hit by his karma.

Okay, it's an old 60s slogan, but I couldn't resist it. If you believe in karma – the bad shit you do comes back to you later – then Osama bin Laden's must have been pretty bad.

A son of a wealthy Saudi family, bin Laden embraced a form of fundamentalist Islamic fanaticism that led him to wage jihad, or holy war, against the Soviets in Afghanistan in the 1980s. He then turned on the Afghan rebels' former backer, America. A series of bombings culminated in the attacks of September 11 2001, in which almost 3,000 people were killed.

Bin Laden was killed by US special forces in 2011 – not hiding in a cave but living in a pleasant compound near the Pakistani capital of Islamabad. It's reported he had been watching old videos of his greatest TV appearances.

WHAT A LOAD OF BANKERS

There once were a lot of big banks
That failed to maintain reserve tanks,
And left to posterity
Pain and austerity,
Taking large bailouts with thanks.

The Wall Street Crash of 1929 was, of course, not the last of its kind. At the turn of the last century, those clever chaps in the big merchant banks once more found all sorts of exciting whizz-bang products to sell, which no one really understood. And when in 2008 the bubble burst (as it always does) the banks, having told customers to take responsibility for their debts, were bailed out to the tune of billions of dollars by taxpayers.

The Credit Crunch led to unemployment, unrest and instability. And if that too sounds a bit like the 1930s all over again, don't worry. As Marx said, 'History repeats itself... the first time as tragedy, the second time as farce'. So this time instead of fascism we seem to have got farcism – good for limericks at least.

TO THE FUTURE

So now that's enough of the past
We've got to the present at last.
The next stage of history
Though still a mystery
Rushes towards us quite fast.

As Bob Dylan so wisely observed in 'The Times They Are a-Changin',
'The present now will later be past'. You could go even further and
point out that even the future yet to come will later be past.

News is the first draft of history. Which means it probably
deserves to be crumpled up and tossed in the waste-bin of
posterity. Or, these days, to linger somewhere on a hard drive or
cloud, accessible only when someone tries to trace prior versions.
Or doesn't bother, because the second, third and fourth drafts
are better.

So you could say that for the past few years I've been working
on the first draft of limerick history, by writing limericks on the
day's news events – a few of which have made their way into the
last chapters here.

ACKNOWLEDGEMENTS

A number of women and blokes
Helped with the history and jokes.
But if this book makes
Horrendous mistakes
Blame me – not these innocent folks!

I'd like to thank everyone who's encouraged my limericking by following, retweeting, favouriting, liking and sharing twitmericks on Twitter, Facebook and Wordpress.

Historians, poets and rhymers in all generations of my family – including my mother Anna Davin, father Luke Hodgkin, and daughters Rosa and Eva – provided inspiration and help.

Shadi Doostdar, Judy Henry and Jeremy Gavron all helped me to get from the idea of a book to the reality, and Katie Cowan and Malcolm Croft at Portico made it work.

Geraldine Holden is a constant source of support, who helps provide rhyme and reason.

ABOUT MICK

Mick Twister is a journalist and crossword compiler. His name is an anagram of 'twitmericks'.

If you can take any more, you can follow @twitmericks on Twitter, or browse through past news limericks at twitmericks.com.